*"Knowledge is of no value
unless you put it into practice."*

-Anton Pavlovich Chekhov

1 EXERCISE:

PROBLEM: How would you fix the following code?

```html
<html>
 <head>
  <title>My title</title>
 </head>
 <body>
  <h1>Hello!</h1>
  <p>Some text</p>
 </body>
 <script>
  alert("It works!");
 </script>
</html>
```

WRITE YOUR ANSWER BELOW.

```
1 <html>
2 <head>
3
4 </head>     <title>
5 <body>
6       <h1></h1>
7 (
8       <p></p>
  <script> </script>
  </body
```

2 EXERCISE:

PROBLEM: How could you make this code work with http and https?

```
<html>
 <head>
  <title>My title</title>
  <script src="http://example.com/script.js"/>
 </head>
 <body></body>
</html>
```

SHOW YOUR ANSWER BELOW:

```
1
2
3
4
5
6
7
```

3   EXERCISE:

PROBLEM: With console.log print the first lines of the song 'Hello Dolly', or a different song if you don't know that one.

YOUR CODE:

```
1
2
3
4
5
6
7
```

4 EXERCISE:

PROBLEM: Print first lines of the Hello Dolly song with one console.log execution.

YOUR CODE:

```
1
2
3
4
5
6
7
```

5   EXERCISE:

PROBLEM: There is a special operator *typeof* that is used to detect the type of a variable. Use *typeof* to determine the type of the following variables:

typeof window; // object

```
var a = 10;
var b = 10.0;
var c = "10";
var d = '10';
var e = a;
var f;
```

YOUR CODE:

```
1
2
3
4
5
6
7
```

6   EXERCISE:

PROBLEM: What do you think the type of the following variables are? Use *typeof* to check your answers.

```
var a = function () {
  return 10;
};
var b = a();
var c = 'a()';
var d = [ 10 ];
var e = { 10: a() };
```

YOUR CODE:

```
1
2
3
4
5
6
7
```

7   EXERCISE:

PROBLEM: What are the values of the variables a,b, and c after the script executes?

```
var a = [1, 2, 3];
var b = a;
var c = a[0];
a[0] = 10;
```

YOUR CODE:

```
1
2
3
4
5
6
7
```

8 EXERCISE:

PROBLEM: Why doesn't this script work like expected?

```
var alex = { name: "Alex", age: 22 };
var stan = alex;
stan["name"] = "Stan"
console.log(stan);
console.log(alex); // Hey! My name is Alex
```

FIX THE ISSUE:

```
1
2
3
4
5
6
7
```

9 EXERCISE:

PROBLEM: What are the values of a and b after script execution? Test yourself using the console.

```
var a = 0;
var b = ++a;
a = a++;
```

YOUR CODE:

```
1
2
3
4
5
6
7
```

10 EXERCISE:

PROBLEM:

What are the values of a, b and c after script execution? Test yourself using the console.

```
var a = 0;
var b = a++;
var c = --b;
a = a++ + ++c + b++ + c + b;
```

YOUR CODE:

```
1
2
3
4
5
6
7
```

11 EXERCISE:

PROBLEM: What are the values of a and b after script execution? Test yourself using the console.

```
var a = 1;
var b = ++a;
a *= 2;
b *= a++;
```

YOUR CODE:

```
1
2
3
4
5
6
7
```

PROBLEM: Using the bitwise operator left shift, '<<' write the solution to the "power of two" problem.

YOUR CODE:

```
1
2
3
4
5
6
7
```

13 EXERCISE:

PROBLEM: What is the result of this expression? Test yourself using the console.

~10 | (2 & 3)

YOUR CODE:

```
1
2
3
4
5
6
7
```

14 EXERCISE:

PROBLEM: Using the XOR operator swap the values of a and b:

```
var a = 1;
var b = 100;
// Write code here
console.log(a); // 100
console.log(b); // 1
```

YOUR CODE:

```
1
2
3
4
5
6
7
```

15 EXERCISE:

PROBLEM: What is the result of the following statement?

3 << 2 - 1;

YOUR CODE:

```
1
2
3
4
5
6
7
```

16 EXERCISE:

PROBLEM: How would you modify the following code so that the result is 1?

```
var a = 2;
var b = 4;
var c = 7;
a * b / c++;
```

YOUR CODE:

```
1
2
3
4
5
6
7
```

17 EXERCISE:

PROBLEM: Fix following code

document[getElementById("bold")]["innerHTML"] = "test";

YOUR CODE:

```
1
2
3
4
5
6
7
```

18 EXERCISE:

PROBLEM: Define a variable, str, that contains a multiline string:

YOUR CODE:

```
1
2
3
4
5
6
7
```

19 EXERCISE:

PROBLEM: What do the following statements return?

"5" + 6
5 + "6"
5 + ("-6")
5 + (-"6")

YOUR CODE:

```
1
2
3
4
5
6
7
```

20 EXERCISE:

PROBLEM: How would you change the last line of the following script to print out the string "12"?

```
var a = 1;
var b = 2;
console.log(a + b);
```

YOUR CODE:

```
1
2
3
4
5
6
7
```

21 EXERCISE:

PROBLEM: What are the values of the boolean variables st1, st2, st3, and st4 after the script executes?

```
var a = 10;
var b = "10";
var c = [ 10 ];
var d = [ 10 ];
var st1 = (a == b);
var st2 = (a === b);
var st3 = (c == d);
var st4 = (c === d);
```

YOUR CODE:

```
1
2
3
4
5
6
7
```

22 EXERCISE:

PROBLEM: Because the numbers are saved in memory as floats with extra precision causing an unexpected round-off error.

1/2 + 1/3 == 2/3
0.1111111111 * 3 == 0.333333333

YOUR CODE:

```
1
2
3
4
5
6
7
```

23 EXERCISE:

PROBLEM: You are in a bar and you decide to buy a drink. You find money in your pocket and place it in a numeric variable, *cache*. The drink prices are $20 for scotch, $10 for vodka, and $5 for beer. Using an elif statement, write a script to purchase the most expensive drink possible using the amount of money you have in *cache*.

YOUR CODE:

```
1
2
3
4
5
6
7
```

24 EXERCISE:

PROBLEM: Using a *switch* statement get a variable and print either its numerical value if possible or "object()" otherwise. Use *typeof* for this, E.g. "4" returns 4, "10.5" returns 10.5, "string", returns object.

YOUR CODE:

```
1
2
3
4
5
6
7
```

PROBLEM:

Write a loop printing all the numbers from 1 to 100 adding "foo" if the number is divisible by 2, "bar" if divisible by 3, and "foobar" if divisible by 6. The output for the first ten numbers should be:

1

2 foo

3 bar

4 foo

5

6 foobar

7

8 foo

9 bar

10 foo

YOUR CODE:

```
1
2
3
4
5
6
7
```

26 EXERCISE:

PROBLEM: Write a function returning the type of the variable

YOUR CODE:

```
1
2
3
4
5
6
7
```

27 EXERCISE:

PROBLEM: You are a robot sitting on the top left corner of a grid, NxM.
You can only move in two directions, right and down. Write a
function returning the number of possible paths there are to the
bottom right hand corner:

YOUR CODE:

```
1
2
3
4
5
6
7
```

28 EXERCISE:

PROBLEM:

Rewrite the following using only one block:

```
if (a) {
 if (b) {
   return "b";
 }
 return "a";
} else {
 return "b";
}
```

YOUR CODE:

```
1
2
3
4
5
6
7
```

29 EXERCISE:

PROBLEM: Rewrite this one without using if/else blocks:

```
var abs = function (a) {
 if (a > 0) {
  return a;
 } else if (a < 0) {
  return -a;
 } else {
  return 0;
 }
}
```

YOUR CODE:

```
1
2
3
4
5
6
7
```

PROBLEM: Add a method, gotoAndPlay to the video object below:

```
video = {
 src: "video.mp4",
 goto: function (frame) {
   console.log("on frame " + frame);
 },
 play: function () {
   console.log("playing" + this.src);
 }
};
```

YOUR CODE:

```
1
2
3
4
5
6
7
```

31 EXERCISE:

PROBLEM: You can use the this keyword to reference the current object from an object method. Use this to change the video. gotoAndPlay method from the previous exercise to fix the following code:

```
video2 = video;
video2.src = "video2.mp4";
video2.gotoAndPlay(10);
```

YOUR CODE:

```
1
2
3
4
5
6
7
```

PROBLEM:

What is the output of following code? Test yourself via console

```javascript
var fn = function () {
  console.log("1");
};
fn();
function fn() {
  console.log("2");
};
fn();

function fn2() {
  console.log("2");
};
fn2();
var fn2 = function () {
  console.log("1");
};
fn2();
```

YOUR CODE:

```
1
2
3
4
5
6
7
```

33 EXERCISE:

PROBLEM: Make this function self-excecuting

```
var num = 10;
function selfExcecute() {
 console.log(num);
};
```

YOUR CODE:

```
1
2
3
4
5
6
7
```

34 EXERCISE:

PROBLEM: Add an argument, 'num' to the function from the previous example to make its definition local and not global, keeping the output the same:

YOUR CODE:

```
1
2
3
4
5
6
7
```

35   EXERCISE:

PROBLEM: What is the output of the following code? Test yourself via console

```
var i = 5;
var counter = function () {
 while (i++ < 10) {
   console.log(i);
  }
};
counter();
console.log(i);
```

YOUR CODE:

```
1
2
3
4
5
6
7
```

36 EXERCISE:

PROBLEM:

Fix the following code so that it counts from 1 to 10:

```
var counter = function (i) {
 console.log(i);
 if (i >= 10) return;
 counter(i++);
};
counter(1);
```

YOUR CODE:

```
1
2
3
4
5
6
7
```

PROBLEM: Fix the following:

```
var powers = [];
for (i = 0; i <= 10; i++) {
  powers[i] = function () {
    console.log(i * i);
  };
}
powers[5](); //should be 25
```

YOUR CODE:

```
1
2
3
4
5
6
7
```

PROBLEM:

Fix the code:

```
fn();
var fn = function () {
  console.log("It works!");
}
```

YOUR CODE:

```
1
2
3
4
5
6
7
```

39 EXERCISE:

PROBLEM: What is the output of following code? Test yourself via console

```
var cookies;
var darkside = function () {
 var lightside = function () {
  cookies = false;
 };
 cookies = true;
 lightside();
};
darkside();
console.log(cookies);
```

YOUR CODE:

```
1
2
3
4
5
6
7
```

PROBLEM: Finish the following code:

```
var c;
var fn = function () {
  if (c === undefined) {
    return function (i) {
      c = i;
    };
  }
  return c;
};
// Add something here
fn(); // Should return 10
```

YOUR CODE:

```
1
2
3
4
5
6
7
```

41 EXERCISE:

function wran) hind('onReset', function () {

PROBLEM: What is the length of following array? Test yourself via console

var a = [];
a[10] = 10;

YOUR CODE:

```
1
2
3
4
5
6
7
```

42   EXERCISE:

PROBLEM: Write a function that prints all the array values to the console.

```
var printArray = function (a) {
 var i;
 for (i = 0; i < a.length; i++) {
  console.log(a[i]);
 }
};
```

YOUR CODE:

```
1
2
3
4
5
6
7
```

43 EXERCISE:

PROBLEM: Fix the following code:

```
var powerArray = function (a) {
 var i;
 for (i = 0; i < a.length; i++) {
  a[i * i] = a[i] * a[i];
 }
 return a;
};
powerArray([0, 1, 2, 3])[9]; // Should be 9
```

YOUR CODE:

```
1
2
3
4
5
6
7
```

44 EXERCISE:

PROBLEM: What is the output of following code?

a = [1, 2, 3, 4, 5];
console.log(a.shift(), a.pop(), a.push(6), a.unshift(0), a);

YOUR CODE:

```
1
2
3
4
5
6
7
```

45 EXERCISE:

PROBLEM: Use a *for* loop and *push* to create an array containing the numbers 1 to 10:

YOUR CODE:

```
1
2
3
4
5
6
7
```

PROBLEM: Modify your answer from the previous exercise changing only the loop to input the numbers 10 to 1:

YOUR CODE:

```
1
2
3
4
5
6
7
```

47 EXERCISE:

PROBLEM: Fix the following code to have both functions executed on click:

```html
<html>
 <head>
 </head>
 <body>
  <button id="button">Click me</button>
  <script>
   var foo = function () {
    console.log("foo");
   };
   var bar = function () {
    console.log("bar");
   };
   document.getElementById("button").onclick = foo;
   document.getElementById("button").onclick = bar;
  </script>
 </body>
</html>
```

48 EXERCISE:

PROBLEM: Using the DOMContentLoaded event on the document object fix the following:

```
<html>
 <head>
  <script>
   getElementById("input").value = "123";
  </script>
 </head>
 <body>
  <input id="input"></input>
 </body>
</html>
```

49 EXERCISE:

PROBLEM: Modify your code from the previous exercise to make the an integers only field, using keypress, keyup, and keydown events.

PROBLEM:

To the following write an 'add' method body:

```
var Users = {};
Users.list = [];
Users.add = function (name) {
  // Put your code here
};
Users.add("John");
Users.add("Mary");
console.log(Users.list); // Should be [ "John", "Mary" ]
```

YOUR CODE:

```
1
2
3
4
5
6
7
```

PROBLEM: Change the method from the previous exercise to work with chain notation:

Users.add("John").add("Mary");
console.log(Users.list); // Should be ["John", "Mary"]

YOUR CODE:

```
1
2
3
4
5
6
7
```

52 EXERCISE:

PROBLEM: Add a 'print' method to the previous exercise's code that prints all users.

YOUR CODE:

```
1
2
3
4
5
6
7
```

53 EXERCISE:

PROBLEM: Fix the following code:

```
var User = function (name) {
 this.name = name;
};
var john = User("john");
console.log(john.name);
```

YOUR CODE:

```
1
2
3
4
5
6
7
```

PROBLEM:

A *singleton* is a constructor that has exactly one object. Fix the code below to make the constructor work like a singleton:

```
var Singleton = function () {
};
var a = new Singleton();
var b = new Singleton();
console.log(a === b); // Should be true
```

YOUR CODE:

```
1
2
3
4
5
6
7
```

PROBLEM: Write a constructor 'Family' that checks the value of the surname field and if matching returns the same instance of the object:

var john = { name: "john", surname: "white" }

var mike = { name: "mike", surname: "black" }

var linda = { name: "linda", surname: "white" }

console.log(new Family(john) === new Family(linda)); // Should be true

console.log(new Family(john) === new Family(mike)); // Should be false

YOUR CODE:

```
1
2
3
4
5
6
7
```

PROBLEM:

What's wrong with the code below?

```
var Users = function () {
};
Users.prototype.list = [];
Users.prototype.add = function (name) {
 this.list.push(name);
 return this;
};
```

YOUR CODE:

```
1
2
3
4
5
6
7
```

57 EXERCISE:

PROBLEM: Finish the Users object rewrite:

YOUR CODE:

```
1
2
3
4
5
6
7
```

PROBLEM:

The following constructor counts the number of instances it has. Fix the code to make it work correctly:

```
var Counter = function () {
  this.count++;
};
Counter.prototype.count = 0;
new Counter();
new Counter();
console.log((new Counter()).count); // Should be 3
```

YOUR CODE:

```
1
2
3
4
5
6
7
```

59 EXERCISE:

PROBLEM: Write a function to calculate the sum of the numbers 1 to N:

YOUR CODE:

```
1
2
3
4
5
6
7
```

60 EXERCISE:

PROBLEM: loop:

YOUR CODE:

```
1
2
3
4
5
6
7
```

PROBLEM: The Fibonacci sequence is often used in math. The first two numbers are 1 and 1 and each subsequent number is the sum of the previous two. Write a function to calculate the Nth number of the Fibonacci sequence:

YOUR CODE:

```
1
2
3
4
5
6
7
```

62 EXERCISE:

PROBLEM: Do the previous exercise without using loops.

YOUR CODE:

```
1
2
3
4
5
6
7
```

63 EXERCISE:

PROBLEM: A prime number is a natural number greater than or equal to 1 that can only be divided by one and itself. Write a function to test if a number is prime:

YOUR CODE:

```
1
2
3
4
5
6
7
```

64 EXERCISE:

PROBLEM: Bertrand's postulate states that for any integer N > 3, there is always at least one prime number between N and 2N. Write a function that returns the prime number(s) given the integer N:

YOUR CODE:

```
1
2
3
4
5
6
7
```

65 EXERCISE:

PROBLEM: Write a function given B and N and returning the B raised to the power of N.

YOUR CODE:

```
1
2
3
4
5
6
7
```

66 EXERCISE:

PROBLEM: Write a function like in the previous exercise except that it uses big numbers and returns only the last number of the power. E.g. power_number(10,1000) should return 0.

YOUR CODE:

```
1
2
3
4
5
6
7
```

67 EXERCISE:

PROBLEM: Check and see if it's possible that a, b, and c could be sides of a
triangle:

YOUR CODE:

```
1
2
3
4
5
6
7
```

68 EXERCISE:

PROBLEM: There are two circles with properties x, y, and r. Write a
function returning how many common points they share(0, 1, 2,
or infinity):

PROBLEM: A palindrome is a word that reads the same forwards and backwards such as level, noon, racecar, etc. Write a function to test if a word is a palindrome:

YOUR CODE:

```
1
2
3
4
5
6
7
```

PROBLEM:

The shell game has three shells and a small ball. The game begins with a ball under the first shell. The shells are then shuffled as follows:

A) Swap shell 1 and 2

B) Swap shell 2 and 3

C) Swap shell 1 and 3

Write a function returning the number of the shell that covers the ball given a move sequence string(for example: "CBABCACCC" the function should return 1):

PROBLEM: Write a simple strings archiver that changes a repeating letter to the letter followed by the number of times it repeats. E.g. "veeeeeeeryyyyyyy looooooooooooooooooong teext should return "ve7ry6 lo18ng te2xt":

YOUR CODE:

```
1
2
3
4
5
6
7
```

72 EXERCISE:

PROBLEM: Write an expander for the previous exercise:

YOUR CODE:

```
1
2
3
4
5
6
7
```

73 EXERCISE:

PROBLEM: Write a function that accepts an array and returns a reversed
copy of the array:

YOUR CODE:

```
1
2
3
4
5
6
7
```

PROBLEM: Now using the last exercise write a function that actually reverses the array and returns it:

var arr = [1, 2, 3];
reverse(arr);
console.log(arr); // [3, 2, 1]

YOUR CODE:

```
1
2
3
4
5
6
7
```

75 EXERCISE:

PROBLEM: Add the function form the previous exercise to the Array
prototype:

var arr = [1, 2, 3];
arr.reverse();
console.log(arr); // [3, 2, 1]

YOUR CODE:

```
1
2
3
4
5
6
7
```

76 EXERCISE:

PROBLEM: A chessboard consists of 64 squares alternating black and white. Each square can be pointed to with a letter, a to h, and a number, 1 to 8. Write a function returning the color of the square by its notated location. E.g. "c3" should return "black":

PROBLEM: Write a function that takes an array of numbers and returns an array with those numbers sorted from smallest to largest:

YOUR CODE:

```
1
2
3
4
5
6
7
```

PROBLEM: Modify the previous function to sort the numbers from largest to smallest:

YOUR CODE:

```
1
2
3
4
5
6
7
```

PROBLEM:

Using a function *delta* that takes two arguments and returns their difference rewrite the sort function from the previous exercise to sort based on delta:

```
var delta = function (a, b) {
  return a - b;
};
arr = [5, 8, 2, 10];
console.log(sort(arr, delta)); // [2, 5, 8, 10]
```

YOUR CODE:

```
1
2
3
4
5
6
7
```

80 EXERCISE:

PROBLEM: Modify the previous exercise's delta function to make the function sort from larger to smaller:

YOUR CODE:

```
1
2
3
4
5
6
7
```

81 EXERCISE:

PROBLEM:

Rewrite the delta function from the previous exercise to sort strings based on length:

arr = ["bird", "apple", "application", "acid", "bicycle", "sun", "app"];
console.log(sort(arr, delta)); // ["sun", "app", "bird", "acid", "apple", "bicycle", "application"]

YOUR CODE:

```
1
2
3
4
5
6
7
```

PROBLEM: Rewrite the delta function from the previous exercise to sort strings alphabetically:

arr = ["bird", "apple", "application", "acid", "bicycle", "sun", "app"];
console.log(sort(arr, delta)); // ["acid", "app", "apple", "application", "bicycle", "bird", "sun"]

YOUR CODE:

```
1
2
3
4
5
6
7
```

83 EXERCISE:

PROBLEM:

Rewrite the delta function from the previous exercise to make the function sort strings by size, then if the lengths are equal, alphabetically:

arr = ["bird", "apple", "application", "acid", "bicycle", "sun", "app"];
console.log(sort(arr, delta)); // ["app", "sun", "acid", "bird", "apple", "bicycle", "application"]

YOUR CODE:

```
1
2
3
4
5
6
7
```

PROBLEM: Math.round is a function returning an integer closest to the given integer. Write a function that returns an number rounded to N decimal:

YOUR CODE:

```
1
2
3
4
5
6
7
```

PROBLEM: The Math.random method returns a random number between 0 and 1. Write a function returning a random integer between N and M:

YOUR CODE:

```
1
2
3
4
5
6
7
```

EXERCISE:

PROBLEM: A good randomization function should return close to the same percentage for each possible result for a huge amount of tries. Write code printing statistics for your random function:

YOUR CODE:

```
1
2
3
4
5
6
7
```

87 EXERCISE:

PROBLEM: Write a function that generates a random password. The password should be an eight character long string of lowercase letters and numbers:

YOUR CODE:

```
1
2
3
4
5
6
7
```

88 EXERCISE:

PROBLEM: The trim function is common in many programming languages. It removes whitespace from both sides of a string. Write your own implementation of the trim function:

YOUR CODE:

```
1
2
3
4
5
6
7
```

PROBLEM: It's common to replace white spaces in URLs with underscores. Write a function that replaces whitespace in a string with an '_':

underscore("hello world   !"); // "hello_world_!"

YOUR CODE:

```
1
2
3
4
5
6
7
```

PROBLEM: Write a function returning intersection of two arrays.

intersection([1, 2, 3, 4], [1, 3, 5]); // [1, 3]

YOUR CODE:

```
1
2
3
4
5
6
7
```

PROBLEM: Write a class *Inspector* with a method inspect that prints all instance's fields.

var i = new Inspector();
i.foo = "foo";
i.bar = "bar";
i.inspect(); // foo, bar

YOUR CODE:

```
1
2
3
4
5
6
7
```

92 EXERCISE:

PROBLEM: Add a method *run* to the class from the previous exercise that causes the class to execute all its methods:

```
var i = new Inspector();
i.foo = "foo";
i.bar = function () {
  console.log("bar");
};
i.run(); // bar
```

YOUR CODE:

```
1
2
3
4
5
6
7
```

93 EXERCISE:

PROBLEM: Modify `run` method from previous exercise to make it note the time of each method excecution. Use (new Date()).getTime() to have retrieve timestamp.

```
var i = new Inspector();
i.foo = function () {
  var i;
  for (i = 0; i < 1000000; i++);
};
i.bar = function () {
  var i;
  for (i = 0; i < 10000000; i++);
};
i.run(); // foo: 2, bar: 7
```

YOUR CODE:

```
1
2
3
4
5
6
7
```

PROBLEM: Write a method *last* that works on an array returning its last element:

[1, 2, 3].last(); // 3

YOUR CODE:

```
1
2
3
4
5
6
7
```

95 EXERCISE:

PROBLEM:

Write a method *sample* that works on an array returning a random element:

[1, 2, 3].sample(); // 2

YOUR CODE:

```
1
2
3
4
5
6
7
```

PROBLEM: Write a method that works on an array returning a shuffled copy:

[1, 2, 3, 4, 5].shuffle(); // [4, 3, 5, 2, 1]

YOUR CODE:

```
1
2
3
4
5
6
7
```

97   EXERCISE:

PROBLEM: Write a *method* clone that works on an object and returns a copy:

```
var alex = { name: "Alex", age: 22 };
var stan = alex.clone();
stan.name = "Stan"
console.log(stan.name); // "Stan"
console.log(alex.name); // "Alex"
```

YOUR CODE:

```
1
2
3
4
5
6
7
```

PROBLEM:

Modify the *clone* method from the previous exercise to work with nested objects:

```
var alex = { name: "Alex", age: 22, skills: { js: 5, php: 3 } };
var stan = alex.clone();
stan.skills.php = 5;
console.log(stan.skills); // { js: 5, php: 5 }
console.log(alex.skills); // { js: 5, php: 3 }
```

YOUR CODE:

```
1
2
3
4
5
6
7
```

PROBLEM:

Write a method *once* that works with functions that returns a function that can only be called once:

```
var foo = function () {
  console.log("foo");
};
foo = foo.once();
foo(); // foo
foo(); // nothing
```

YOUR CODE:

```
1
2
3
4
5
6
7
```

100 EXERCISE:

PROBLEM: Write a method chain that works with functions returning
specified functions called in a chain:

```
var foo = function () {
  console.log("foo");
};
var bar = function () {
  console.log("bar");
};
var buz = function () {
  console.log("buz");
};
foo.chain(bar).chain(buz)(); // foo, bar, buz
```

YOUR CODE:

```
1
2
3
4
5
6
7
```

```
_loadIframe: function() {
    var coming = F.coming,
        iframe = $(coming.tpl.iframe.replace(/\{rnd\
            .attr('scrolling', isTouch ? 'auto' : co
            .attr('src', coming.href);
oad: function () {
coming    = F.coming,
previous
placehold    lder',              // This helps IE
current,                         $(coming.wrap).bind('onReset', function () {
content,                             try {
type,                                    $(this).find('iframe').hide().attr('src
scrolling,                           } catch (e) {}
href,
embed;
```

ANSWERS:

EXERCISE 1

```
<html>
 <head>
  <title>My title</title>
 </head>
 <body>
  <h1>Hello!</h1>
  <p>Some text</p>
 <script>alert("It works!");</script>
 </body>
</html>
```

EXERCISE 2

```
<html>
 <head>
  <title>My title</title>
  <script src="//example.com/script.js"/>
 </head>
 <body></body>
</html>
```

EXERCISE 3

```
console.log(20);
```

EXERCISE 4

```
console.log("I said hello, Dolly,\nWell, hello, Dolly\nIt's so nice to
have you back where you belong");
```

EXERCISE 8

```
var alex = { name: "Alex", age: 22 };
var stan = { name: "Stan", age: 22 };
console.log(stan);
console.log(alex);
```

ANSWERS:

```
_loadIframe: function() {
    var coming = F.coming,
    iframe = $(coming.tpl.iframe.replace(/\{rnd\}/
        .attr('scrolling', isTouch ? 'auto' : com
        .attr('src', coming.href);

    // This helps IE
    $(coming.wrap).bind('onReset', function () {
        try {
            $(this).find('iframe').hide().attr('src'
        } catch (e) {}
```

EXERCISE 12   1 << 10 // 10 is an exponent

EXERCISE 14
```
var alex = { name: "Alex", age: 22 };
var stan = { name: "Stan", age: 22 };
console.log(stan);
console.log(alex);
```

EXERCISE 16   a * b / ++c;

EXERCISE 17   document.getElementById("bold")["innerHTML"] = "test";

EXERCISE 18   var str = "First line\nSecond line";

EXERCISE 20   "" + a + b

EXERCISE 22   *Because numbers in the memory are saving as float with some accuracy. So it's just round-off error.*

_loadIframe: function() {
        var coming = F.coming,
            iframe = $(coming.tpl.iframe.replace(/\{rnd\
                .attr('scrolling', isTouch ? 'auto' : co
                .attr('src', coming.href);

        // This helps IE
        $(coming.wrap).bind('onReset', function () {
            try {
                $(this).find('iframe').hide().attr('src
            } catch (e) {}

ANSWERS:

EXERCISE 23

```
if (cache >= 20) {
  console.log("scotch");
} else if (cache >= 10) {
  console.log("vodka");
} else if (bear >= 5) {
  console.log("bear");
} else {
  console.log("go home");
}
```

EXERCISE 24

```
switch (typeof variable) {
  case "string":
    variable = +variable;
    if (variable === NaN) {
      console.log("object");
      break;
    }
    console.log(variable);
  case "number":
    console.log(variable);
    break;
  default:
    console.log("object");
}
```

EXERCISE 25

```
for (var i = 1; i <= 100; i++) {
  if (i % 6 === 0) {
    console.log(i + " foobar");
  } else if (i % 2 === 0) {
    console.log(i + " foo");
  } else if (i % 3 === 0) {
    console.log(i + " bar");
  } else {
    console.log(i);
  }
}
```

EXERCISE 26

```
var typeOf = function (v) {
  return typeof v;
};
```

EXERCISE 27

```
var paths = function (n, m) {
  if (n === 1) return 1;
  if (m === 1) return 1;
  return paths(n - 1, m) + paths(n, m - 1);
}
```

EXERCISE 28

```
if (a && !b) {
  return "a";
}
return "b";
```

```
oad: function () {
  coming    = F.coming,
  previous
  placehold
  current,
  content,
  type,
  scrolling,
  href,
  embed;
```

```
_loadIframe: function() {
  var coming = F.coming,
    iframe = $(coming.tpl.iframe.replace(/\{rnd\
      .attr('scrolling', isTouch ? 'auto' : cc
      .attr('src', coming.href);

  // This helps IE
  $(coming.wrap).bind('onReset', function () {
    try {
      $(this).find('iframe').hide().attr('src
    } catch (e) {}
```

ANSWERS:

EXERCISE 29

```
var abs = function (a) {
  return (a >= 0) ? a : -a;
};
```

EXERCISE 30

```
video.gotoAndPlay = function (frame) {
  video.goto(frame);
  video.play();
};
```

EXERCISE 31

```
video.gotoAndPlay = function (frame) {
  this.goto(frame);
  this.play();
};
```

EXERCISE 33

```
var num = 10;
(function () {
  console.log(num);
}());
```

EXERCISE 34

```
(function (num) {
  console.log(num);
}(10));
```

EXERCISE 36

```
var counter = function (i) {
  console.log(i);
  if (i >= 10) return;
  counter(++i);
};
counter(1);
```

EXERCISE 37

```
var powers = [];
for (i = 0; i <= 10; i++) {
  powers[i] = (function (i) {
    return function () {
      console.log(i * i);
    };
  }(i));
}
powers[5](); //should be 25
```

EXERCISE 38

```
fn();
function fn() {
  console.log("It works!");
}
```

ANSWERS:

```
oad: function () {
 coming    = F.coming,
 previous
 placehold        lder',
 current,
 content,
 type,
 scrolling,
 href,
 embed;
```

```
  _loadIframe: function() {
    var coming = F.coming,
    iframe = $(coming.tpl.iframe.replace(/\{rnd\
      .attr('scrolling', isTouch ? 'auto' : co
      .attr('src', coming.href);

  // This helps IE
  $(coming.wrap).bind('onReset', function () {
    try {
      $(this).find('iframe').hide().attr('src
    } catch (e) {}
```

EXERCISE 40

```
var c;
var fn = function () {
 if (c === undefined) {
  return function (i) {
   c = i;
  };
 }
 return c;
};
fn()(10);
fn(); // Should return 10
```

EXERCISE 43

```
var powerArray = function (a) {
 var i, l = a.length;
 for (i = 0; i < l; i++) {
  a[i * i] = a[i] * a[i];
 }
 return a;
};
powerArray([0, 1, 2, 3])[9]; // Should be 9
```

EXERCISE 45

```
var i, a = [];
for (i = 1; i <= 10; i++) {
 a.push(i);
}
```

EXERCISE 46

```
var i, a = [];
for (i = 1; i <= 10; i++) {
 a.unshift(i);
}
```

EXERCISE 47

```
<html>
 <head>
 </head>
 <body>
  <button id="button">Click me</button>
  <script>
   var foo = function () {
    console.log("foo");
   };
   var bar = function () {
    console.log("bar");
   };
   document.getElementById("button").addEventListener("click", foo);
   document.getElementById("button").addEventListener("click", bar);
  </script>
 </body>
</html>
```

```
oad: function () {
coming   = F.coming,
previous
placehold        lder',
current,
content,
type,
scrolling,
href,
embed;
```

```
_loadIframe: function() {
    var coming = F.coming,
        iframe = $(coming.tpl.iframe.replace(/\{rnd\
            .attr('scrolling', isTouch ? 'auto' : co
            .attr('src', coming.href);

    // This helps IE
    $(coming.wrap).bind('onReset', function () {
        try {
            $(this).find('iframe').hide().attr('src
        } catch (e) {}
```

ANSWERS:

EXERCISE 48

```html
<html>
 <head>
  <script>
   document.addEventListener("DOMContentLoaded", function () {
    document.getElementById("input").value = "123";
   });
  </script>
 </head>
 <body>
  <input id="input"></input>
 </body>
</html>
```

ming = F.coming,
evious
aceholder',
irrent,
ontent,
ype,
crolling,
ref,
mbed;

_loadIframe: function() {
    var coming = F.coming,
        iframe = $(coming.tpl.iframe.replace(/\{rnd\}/
            .attr('scrolling', isTouch ? 'auto' : comi
            .attr('src', coming.href);

    // This helps IE
    $(coming.wrap).bind('onReset', function () {
        try {
            $(this).find('iframe').hide().attr('src',
        } catch (e) {}

EXERCISE 49

```html
<html>
 <head>
  <script>
   document.addEventListener("DOMContentLoaded", function () {
    var html = "";
    var input = document.getElementById("input");
    var listener = function () {
     var new_html = input.value;
     if (new_html == +new_html) {
      html = new_html;
      return;
     }
     input.value = html;
    };
    input.addEventListener("keypress", listener);
    input.addEventListener("keyup", listener);
    input.addEventListener("keydown", listener);
   });
  </script>
 </head>
 <body>
  <input id="input"></input>
 </body>
</html>
```

EXERCISE 50

```js
Users.add = function (name) {
 this.list.push(name);
};
```

```
oad: function () {
  coming    = F.coming,
  previous                                                       _loadIframe: function() {
  placeholder                                                       var coming = F.coming,
```
ANSWERS:
```
  current,                                                       iframe = $(coming.tpl.iframe.replace(/\{rnd\
  content,                                                       .attr('scrolling', isTouch ? 'auto' : cc
  type,                                                          .attr('src', coming.href);
  scrolling,
  href,                                                    // This helps IE
  embed;                                                    $(coming.wrap).bind('onReset', function () {
                                                               try {
                                                                 $(this).find('iframe').hide().attr('src
                                                             } catch (e) {}
```

EXERCISE 51

```
Users.add = function (name) {
  this.list.push(name);
  return this;
};
```

EXERCISE 52

```
Users.print = function () {
  var i, l = this.list.length;
  for (i = 0; i < l; i++) {
    console.log(this.list[i]);
  }
};
```

EXERCISE 53

```
var User = function (name) {
  this.name = name;
};
var john = new User("john");
console.log(john.name);
```

EXERCISE 54

```
var Singleton = (function () {
  var instance = null;
  return function () {
    if (instance !== null) return instance;
    instance = this;
  };
}());

var a = new Singleton();
var b = new Singleton();
console.log(a === b);
```

```
_loadIframe: function () {
    var coming = F.coming,
        iframe = $(coming.tpl.iframe.replace(/\{rnd\}/
            .attr('scrolling', isTouch ? 'auto' : com
            .attr('src', coming.href);

    // This helps IE
    $(coming.wrap).bind('onReset', function () {
        try {
            $(this).find('iframe').hide().attr('src'
        } catch (e) {}
```

EXERCISE 55

```javascript
var families = {};
var Family = function (user) {
  var surname = user.surname;
  if (families.hasOwnProperty(surname)) {
    return families[surname];
  }
  families[surname] = this;
};
```

EXERCISE 56

The list is the same for all Users instance. So
```javascript
var u1 = new Users();
var u2 = new Users();
u1.add("John").add("Mary");
console.log(u1.list); // ["John", "Mary"]
console.log(u2.list); // ["John", "Mary"], but should be empty!
```

EXERCISE 57

```javascript
var Users = function () {
  this.list = [];
};
Users.prototype.add = function (name) {
  this.list.push(name);
  return this;
};
Users.prototype.print = function () {
  var i, l = this.list.length;
  for (i = 0; i < l; i++) {
    console.log(this.list[i]);
  }
};
```

EXERCISE 58

```
var Counter = function () {
  Counter.prototype.count++;
};
Counter.prototype.count = 0;
new Counter();
new Counter();
console.log((new Counter()).count); // Should be 5
```

EXERCISE 59

```
var sum = function (N) {
  var i, s = 0;
  for (i = 1; i <= N; i++) {
    s += i;
  }
  return s;
};
```

EXERCISE 60

```
var sum = function (N) {
  return N * (1 + (N - 1) / 2); // It's just arithmetic progression with
initial term 1 and step 1
};
```

EXERCISE 61

```
var fibonacci = function (N) {
  var i, seq = [1, 1];
  for (i = 2; i <= N; i++) {
    seq[i] = seq[i - 1] + seq[i - 2];
  }
  return seq[N - 1];
};
```

ANSWERS:

EXERCISE 62

```
var fibonacci = function (N) {
 if (N === 1 || N === 2) return 1;
 return fibonacci(N - 1) + fibonacci(N - 2);
};
```

EXERCISE 63

```
var is_prime = function (N) {
 var i;
 if (N <= 1) return false;
 for (i = 2; i < N; i++) {
  if (N % i === 0) {
   return false;
  }
 }
 return true;
};
```

EXERCISE 64

```
var bertrand = function (N) {
 var i;
 for (i = N + 1; i < 2 * N; i++) {
  if (is_prime(i)) { // We use function from previous exercise
   return i;
  }
 }
};
```

EXERCISE 65

```
var power = function (B, N) {
 var i, r = 1;
 for (i = 1; i <= N; i++) {
  r *= B;
 }
 return r;
};
```

EXERCISE 66

```
var power_number = function (B, N) {
  var i, r = 1;
  for (i = 1; i <= N; i++) {
    r = r * B % 10;
  }
  return r;
};
```

EXERCISE 67

```
var is_triangle = function (a, b, c) {
  if (a + b <= c) return false;
  if (a + c <= b) return false;
  if (b + c <= a) return false;
  return true;
};
```

EXERCISE 68

```
var intersect = function (c1, c2) {
  var dx = c1.x - c2.x;
  var dy = c1.y - c2.y;
  var dd = dx * dx + dy * dy;
  if (dx === 0 && dy === 0 && c1.r === c2.r) return Infinity;
  if (dd <= c1.r * c1.r) {
    // The second circle is inside the first
    if (dd === (c1.r - c2.r) * (c1.r - c2.r)) return 1;
    if (dd < (c1.r - c2.r) * (c1.r - c2.r)) return 0;
    return 2;
  }
  if (dd <= c2.r * c2.r) {
    // The first circle is inside the second
    if (dd === (c1.r - c2.r) * (c1.r - c2.r)) return 1;
    if (dd < (c1.r - c2.r) * (c1.r - c2.r)) return 0;
    return 2;
  }
  if (dd === (c1.r + c2.r) * (c1.r + c2.r)) return 1;
  if (dd > (c1.r + c2.r) * (c1.r + c2.r)) return 0;
  return 2;
};
```

oad: function () {
  coming   = F.coming,
  previous
  placeholder'.
  current,
  content,
  type,
  scrolling,
  href,
  embed;

ANSWERS:

_loadIframe: function() {
    var coming = F.coming,
      iframe = $(coming.tpl.iframe.replace(/\{rnd\
        .attr('scrolling', isTouch ? 'auto' : cc
        .attr('src', coming.href);

    // This helps IE
    $(coming.wrap).bind('onReset', function () {
      try {
        $(this).find('iframe').hide().attr('src
      } catch (e) {}

EXERCISE 69

```
var is_palindrome = function (word) {
  var i, l = word.length;
  for (i = 0; i < l; i++) {
    if (word[i] !== word[l - i - 1]) return false;
  }
  return true;
};
```

EXERCISE 70

```
var shell = function (str) {
  var b = 1; // the number of the shell with the ball
  var i, l = str.length;
  for (i = 0; i < l; i++) {
    switch (str[i]) {
      case 'A':
        if (b === 1) {
          b = 2;
          break;
        }
        if (b === 2) {
          b = 1;
          break;
        }
        break;
      case 'B':
        if (b === 2) {
          b = 3;
          break;
        }
        if (b === 3) {
          b = 2;
          break;
```

```
      }
     break;
    case 'C':
     if (b === 1) {
       b = 3;
       break;
     }
     if (b === 3) {
       b = 1;
       break;
     }
     break;
   }
  }
  return b;
};
```

EXERCISE 71

```
var archiver = function (str) {
 var res = "";
 var char, n = 1;
 var i, l = str.length;
 for (i = 0; i < l; i++) {
  if (char === str[i]) {
   n++;
  } else {
   if (n !== 1) {
    res += n;
   }
   n = 1;
   char = str[i];
   res += char;
  }
 }
 return res;
};
```

EXERCISE 72

```
var unarchiver = function (str) {
  var res = "";
  var char, n = "";
  var i, j, l = str.length;
  for (i = 0; i < l; i++) {
   if (str[i] == +str[i] && str[i] !== " ") { // check if str[i] is a number
    n += str[i];
   } else {
    if (n !== "") {
     n = +n;
     for (j = 1; j < n; j++) {
      res += char;
     }
    }
    n = "";
    char = str[i];
    res += char;
   }
  }
  return res;
};
```

EXERCISE 73

```
var reverse = function (arr) {
  var res = [];
  var i, l = arr.length;
  for (i = l - 1; i >= 0; i--) {
   res.push(arr[i]);
  }
  return res;
};
```

ANSWERS:

EXERCISE 74

```
var reverse = function (arr) {
 var res = [];
 var i, l = arr.length;
 for (i = l - 1; i >= 0; i--) {
  res.push(arr[i]);
 }
 for (i = 0; i < l; i++) {
  arr[i] = res[i];
 }
};
```

EXERCISE 75

```
Array.prototype.reverse = function () {
 var res = [];
 var i, l = this.length;
 for (i = l - 1; i >= 0; i--) {
  res.push(this[i]);
 }
 for (i = 0; i < l; i++) {
  this[i] = res[i];
 }
};
```

EXERCISE 76

```
var color = function (sq) {
var l, n;
switch (sq[0]) {
  case 'a':
   l = 1;
   break;
  case 'b':
   l = 2;
   break;
  case 'c':
   l = 3;
   break;
  case 'd':
   l = 4;
   break;
  case 'e':
   l = 5;
   break;
  case 'f':
   l = 6;
   break;
  case 'g':
   l = 7;
   break;
  case 'h':
   l = 8;
   break;
  }
```

ANSWERS:

```
n = +sq[1];
if ((l + n) % 2 === 0) {
  return "black";
} else {
  return "white";
}
};
```

EXERCISE 77

```
var sort = function (arr) {
  var i, j, l;
  for (i = arr.length - 1; i > 0; i--) {
    for (var j = 0; j < i; j++) {
      if (arr[j] > arr[j + 1]) {
        l = arr[j];
        arr[j] = arr[j + 1];
        arr[j + 1] = l;
      }
    }
  }
  return arr;
};
```

EXERCISE 78

```
var sort = function (arr) {
 var i, j, l;
 for (i = arr.length - 1; i > 0; i--) {
  for (var j = 0; j < i; j++) {
   if (arr[j] < arr[j + 1]) {
    l = arr[j];
    arr[j] = arr[j + 1];
    arr[j + 1] = l;
   }
  }
 }
 return arr;
};
```

EXERCISE 79

```
var sort = function (arr, delta) {
 var i, j, l;
 for (i = arr.length - 1; i > 0; i--) {
  for (var j = 0; j < i; j++) {
   if (delta(arr[j], arr[j + 1]) > 0) {
    l = arr[j];
    arr[j] = arr[j + 1];
    arr[j + 1] = l;
   }
  }
 }
 return arr;
};
```

```
oad: function () {
coming     F.coming,
previous
placeholder         older .
current,
content,
type,
scrolling,
href,
embed;
```

```
_loadIframe: function() {
    var coming = F.coming,
        iframe = $(coming.tpl.iframe.replace(/\{rnd\
            .attr('scrolling', isTouch ? 'auto' : co
            .attr('src', coming.href);

    // This helps IE
    $(coming.wrap).bind('onReset', function () {
        try {
            $(this).find('iframe').hide().attr('src
        } catch (e) {}
```

ANSWERS:

EXERCISE 80
```
var delta = function (a, b) {
  return b - a;
};
```

EXERCISE 81
```
var delta = function (a, b) {
  return a.length - b.length;
};
```

EXERCISE 82
```
var delta = function (a, b) {
  return (a > b ? 1 : 0);
};
```

EXERCISE 83
```
var delta = function (a, b) {
  var r = a.length - b.length;
  if (r !== 0) return r;
  return (a > b ? 1 : 0);
};
```

EXERCISE 84
```
var round = function (num, N) {
  var k = 1, i;
  for (i = 0; i < N; i++) {
   k *= 10;
  }
  return Math.round(num * k) / k;
};
```

EXERCISE 85
```
var rnd = function (N, M) {
  return Math.round(Math.random() * (M - N) + N);
};
```

ANSWERS:

EXERCISE 86

```
var i, stats = [];
for (i = 0; i <= 10; i++) {
 stats.push([0]);
}
for (i = 0; i < 10000; i++) {
 stats[rnd(0, 10)]++;
}
for (i = 0; i <= 10; i++) {
 stats[i] /= 10000;
}
console.log(stats);
```

EXERCISE 87

```
var password = function () {
 var characters = "abcdefghijklmnopqrstuvwxyz0123456789";
 var l = characters.length;
 var i, str = "";
 for (i = 0; i < 8; i++) {
  str += characters[Math.round(Math.random() * l)];
 }
 return str;
};
```

EXERCISE 88

```
var trim = function (str) {
  var res = "";
  var i, j, l = str.length;
  for (i = 0; i < l; i++) {
   if (str[i] !== " ") break;
  }
  for (j = l - 1; j > 0; j--) {
   if (str[j] !== " ") break;
  }
  for (; i <= j; i++) {
   res += str[i];
  }
  return res;
};
```

EXERCISE 89

```
var underscore = function (str) {
  var res = "", u = false;
  var i, l = str.length;
  for (i = 0; i < l; i++) {
   if (str[i] === " ") {
    if (!u) {
     res += "_";
     u = true;
    }
   } else {
    res += str[i];
    u = false;
   }
  }
  return res;
};
```

ANSWERS:

EXERCISE 90

```
var intersection = function (a1, a2) {
  var t, res = [];
  var i1, l1 = a1.length;
  var i2, l2 = a2.length;
  for (i1 = 0; i1 < l1; i1++) {
    t = a1[i1];
    for (i2 = 0; i2 < l2; i2++) {
      if (t === a2[i2]) {
        res.push(t);
        break;
      }
    }
  }
  return res;
};
```

EXERCISE 91

```
var Inspector = function Inspector() {
};
Inspector.prototype.inspect = function () {
  var k;
  for (k in this) if (this.hasOwnProperty(k)) {
    console.log(k);
  }
};
```

EXERCISE 92

```
Inspector.prototype.run = function () {
  var k;
  for (k in this) if (this.hasOwnProperty(k) && typeof this[k] ===
"function") {
    this[k]();
  }
};
```

EXERCISE 93

```
Inspector.prototype.run = function () {
    var k, t;
    for (k in this) if (this.hasOwnProperty(k) && typeof this[k] ===
"function") {
        t = (new Date()).getTime();
        this[k]();
        t = (new Date()).getTime() - t
        console.log(k + ": " + t);
    }
};
```

EXERCISE 94

```
Array.prototype.last = function () {
    return this[this.length - 1];
};
```

EXERCISE 95

```
Array.prototype.sample = function () {
    return this[Math.round(Math.random() * (this.length - 1))];
};
```

EXERCISE 96

```
Array.prototype.shuffle = function () {
  var res = [];
  var t, i, l = this.length;
  for (i = 0; i < l; i++) {
    res.push(this[i]);
  }
  for (i = l - 1; i > 0; i--) {
    var j = Math.round(Math.random() * i);
    t = res[i];
    res[i] = res[j];
    res[j] = t;
  }
  return res;
};
```

EXERCISE 97

```
Object.prototype.clone = function () {
  var k, o = {};
  for (k in this) if (this.hasOwnProperty(k)) {
    o[k] = this[k];
  }
  return o;
};
```

```
oad: function () {
coming    = F.coming,
previous
placeholder',
```
ANSWERS: older',
```
current,
content,
type,
scrolling,
href,
embed;
```
```
_loadIframe: function() {
    var coming = F.coming,
    iframe = $(coming.tpl.iframe.replace(/\{rnd\
        .attr('scrolling', isTouch ? 'auto' : co
        .attr('src', coming.href);

    // This helps IE
    $(coming.wrap).bind('onReset', function () {
        try {
            $(this).find('iframe').hide().attr('src
        } catch (e) {}
```

EXERCISE 98

```javascript
Object.prototype.clone = function () {
  var k, o = {};
  for (k in this) if (this.hasOwnProperty(k)) {
   if (typeof this[k] === "object") {
   console.log(k);
    o[k] = this[k].clone();
   } else {
   console.log(k);
    o[k] = this[k];
   }
  }
  return o;
};
```

EXERCISE 99

```javascript
Function.prototype.once = function (fn) {
  var th = this;
  var called = false;
  return function () {
   if (called) return;
   called = true;
   th();
  };
};
```

EXERCISE 100

```javascript
Function.prototype.chain = function (fn) {
  var th = this;
  return function () {
   th();
   fn();
  };
};
```

Made in the USA
Lexington, KY
29 September 2015